SLOTHS

by Josh Gregory

Children's Press®

An Imprint of Scholastic Inc.

Content Consultant
Dr. Stephen S. Ditchkoff
Professor of Wildlife Sciences
Auburn University
Auburn, Alabama

Photographs ©: cover: Minden Pictures/Superstock, Inc.; 1: Vilainecrevette/Dreamstime; 2 background, 3 background: Mtilghma/Dreamstime; 2 main, 3 main: Luiz Claudio Marigo/Dreamstime; 4, 5 background: Michael & Patricia Fogden/Minden Pictures; 6, 7: Monica Rua/Alamy Images; 8, 9: Luiz Claudio Marigo/Nature Picture Library; 11: age fotostock/Superstock, Inc.; 12, 13: Michael & Patricia Fogden/Minden Pictures; 14, 15: Animals Animals/Superstock, Inc.; 16: Barrett & MacKay/All Canada Photos/Superstock, Inc.; 19: Kjersti Joergensen/Dreamstime; 20, 21: Biosphoto/Superstock, Inc.; 22, 23: Thomas Haupt/imagebro/imageBroker/Superstock, Inc.; 24, 25: Minden Pictures/Superstock, Inc.; 27: Brian Magnier/Dreamstime; 28, 29: Tom McHugh/Science Source; 30, 31: Jaime Chirinos/Science Source; 32: Bill Hatcher/National Geographic Creative; 35: Wayne Lynch All Canada Photos/Superstock, Inc.; 36, 37: Dm9/Zjan/Supplied by Wenn.com/Newscom; 38: Jason Edwards/National Geographic Creative; 39: Jason Edwards/National Geographic Creative; 40, 41: Minden Pictures/Superstock, Inc.; 44 background, 45 background: Mtilghma/Dreamstime; 46: Vilainecrevette/Dreamstime.

Library of Congress Cataloging-in-Publication Data
Gregory, Josh, author.
  Sloths / by Josh Gregory.
    pages cm. — (Nature's children)
  Summary: "This book details the life and habits of sloths"— Provided by publisher.
  Includes bibliographical references and index.
  ISBN 978-0-531-21391-9 (library binding : alk. paper) — ISBN 978-0-531-21494-7 (pbk. : alk. paper)
  1. Sloths—Juvenile literature. I. Title. II. Series: Nature's children (New York, N.Y.)
  QL737.E2G74 2016
  599.3'13—dc23   2014044037

All rights reserved. Published in 2016 by Children's Press, an imprint of Scholastic Inc.

Printed in China 62
SCHOLASTIC, CHILDREN'S PRESS, and associated logos are trademarks and/or registered trademarks of Scholastic Inc.

1 2 3 4 5 6 7 8 9 10 R 25 24 23 22 21 20 19 18 17 16

Sloths

Class	Mammalia
Order	Pilosa
Family	Bradypodidae and Megalonychidae
Genera	2 genera
Species	6 species
World distribution	South America and Central America
Habitat	Dense tropical forests
Distinctive physical characteristics	Long limbs ending in two or three long, pointed claws; thick fur that ranges in color from brown to gray; small head; short tail; three-toed sloths are around 23 inches (58 centimeters) long from nose to tail and weigh roughly 8.75 pounds (4 kilograms); two-toed sloths are usually between 24 and 27 inches (61 and 69 cm) long and weigh about 17.5 pounds (8 kg)
Habits	Uses long limbs to hang from tree branches; spends almost all its time in trees, coming down only around once a week to urinate and defecate; moves very slowly; can move only by crawling when on the ground; mainly solitary except during mating seasons; uses claws to fight off predators; mostly nocturnal
Diet	Mostly leaves; also eats fruit and other plant parts; sometimes eats small animals

Contents

CHAPTER 1

Slow and Steady

The Amazon rain forest is home to the world's largest variety of life, from insects, fish, and mammals to a wide range of plant species. As you make your way through the forest's densely packed trees, you might hear the sound of colorful parrots squawking to one another in the branches above. You also might notice a group of monkeys swinging among the vines or a jaguar creeping along the ground.

If you look hard enough, you might even spot something that looks like a clump of leaves wedged between the branches of a tree. At first, this shape seems perfectly still. But watch long enough, and you might notice it slowly unfolding a long arm and reaching for a nearby branch. It isn't a clump of leaves at all. It's a sloth! The sloth hooks its long claws around the branch and drops down to hang below. It doesn't seem to be in a hurry. Taking its time, it begins to climb along from tree to tree.

A brown-throated three-toed sloth hangs comfortably from a tree in the Amazon rain forest in Brazil.

Forest Dwellers

Sloths are known for their slow, careful movements. No other mammal on Earth moves more slowly. There are several different sloth species. Scientists divide them into two groups, or **genera**: two-toed sloths and three-toed sloths. While these sloths have some differences, they all live in similar homes. In fact, they often occupy the exact same **habitats**.

Sloths live high up in treetops, and they travel by climbing from one tree to another. This lifestyle requires them to live in areas where there is dense tree growth. They are native only to the rain forests of South America and Central America, including the Amazon rain forest.

Two-toed sloths have a wider range than their three-toed cousins. They can be found throughout most of northern South America and extend north into Central America. Three-toed sloths are most often found only in parts of northern South America. Some species, though, extend to other areas. For example, the maned sloth lives farther south, along the Atlantic coast of Brazil.

The maned sloth is one of several different sloth species.

Sizing Up Sloths

There are several differences among sloth genera and species. For example, the main difference between two-toed and three-toed sloths is the number of toes on their front feet. However, all sloths share a similar overall physical appearance. These furry mammals have long limbs to help them climb through the treetops. Each of their toes ends in a long, sharp claw. Sloths also have small, round heads, and short, stubby tails.

Sloths are not very large animals. An average three-toed sloth is around 23 inches (58 centimeters) long from nose to tail. It weighs roughly 8.75 pounds (4 kilograms). Two-toed species tend to be larger and heavier than their relatives. They are usually between 24 and 27 inches (61 and 69 cm) long and weigh about 17.5 pounds (8 kg).

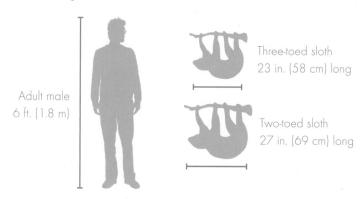

Adult male
6 ft. (1.8 m)

Three-toed sloth
23 in. (58 cm) long

Two-toed sloth
27 in. (69 cm) long

A sloth's arms are slightly longer than its back legs.

CHAPTER 2

Survival Skills

Sloths may not move very fast, but they are experts at traveling through the forest treetops. Unlike most other animals, they do not stand in an upright position. Instead, they spend most of their time hanging upside down from branches. A sloth curls its long, curved claws around branches, and leaves its body hanging below. When it needs to move, the sloth slowly climbs along in this position. It can also climb up by wrapping its legs around vertical tree trunks. Then it takes one slow step at a time. The sloth's grip is extremely strong, and it carefully tests each step before moving forward. As a result, these animals rarely fall from their treetop homes by accident. Sometimes even long after a sloth has died it will still be gripping a branch.

Sloths are very good at swimming. They climb along branches that hang above rivers and drop into the water below. Then they use their long limbs for paddling.

Sloths are surprisingly good swimmers.

A Sloth's Shortcomings

A sloth's body enables it to move through trees easily, but creates a number of difficulties when the animal tries to move along the ground. A sloth's limbs cannot support its body from below. This means the sloth can't stand up to walk or run. Instead, it lies on its belly and reaches out, one arm at a time, to crawl gradually along the ground. The slow, awkward movement leaves the sloth vulnerable to attacks from predators.

Sloths are also lacking when it comes to their senses. Like all animals, sloths rely on their senses to find food, avoid threats, and communicate. However, their eyesight and hearing are not very good. They have small, weak eyes that work best when the light is not too bright. Their ears are very small and mostly hidden beneath fur. Because of these things, a sloth's most important senses are smell and touch. In fact, many experts believe that sloths search out food almost entirely with these two senses.

As slow as sloths are in trees, they are even slower on the ground.

Lunchtime

A sloth's diet is made up almost entirely of leaves. However, sloths also eat other plant parts, including fruit and flower buds. In rare cases, they even eat small animals.

Leaves do not provide a lot of nutrients. This is fine for sloths, as their slow-paced lifestyle does not require a lot of energy. However, they must still eat a lot in order to fuel their bodies and stay healthy. Sloths have especially large stomachs. They eat enough to make sure that their stomachs stay full at all times. As much as a third of a sloth's total weight can come from the food in its belly.

It takes a sloth a lot of time to digest the food it eats. It can be a whole month from the time a sloth eats something until that food passes through the animal's body as waste.

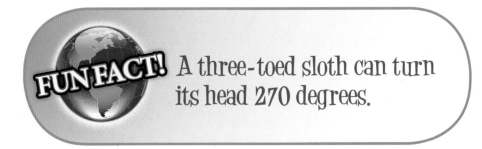

FUN FACT! A three-toed sloth can turn its head 270 degrees.

Sloths can hang from their back legs, leaving their front claws free to grab food.

Fur Features

One of a sloth's most important features is its fur. A sloth has two separate fur layers. On top is a coat of long, shaggy hair in various shades of brown and gray. Underneath is a layer of short black and white hair. Because sloths move so little, algae grow on the outer fur layer. This gives the sloth a slightly greenish color. When a sloth grooms itself, it eats some of the algae. This is an important source of nutrients.

A sloth's fur grows in the opposite direction from how fur grows on all other mammals. On other animals, fur is parted along the animal's back and points around toward the animal's belly. A sloth's fur is parted along its belly and points around toward its back. This makes a lot of sense for an animal that is usually upside down. Such a fur arrangement allows rainwater to run off the sloth's coat when it is hanging in its usual position.

Algae can cause some sloths to turn a bright green color.

Protection from Predators

The rain forests where sloths live are packed with dangerous hunters. For example, big cats such as jaguars and ocelots prey on sloths. So do birds of prey, including certain types of hawks and eagles. Large snakes can also pose a threat.

A sloth's best defense against these powerful predators is to simply avoid being noticed. It can be difficult to spot sloths sitting or hanging completely still among the leaves and branches. Even when they are moving, sloths are often too slow to detect. In addition, the coloring created by green algae on brownish fur blends in perfectly with many trees. This gives sloths excellent camouflage.

Despite their ability to hide, sloths must sometimes defend themselves. This is especially true when they are on the ground, where they have no way to escape. In these situations, the sloth's powerful claws can be used as weapons to fend off attackers. A sloth might also bite predators with its sharp teeth.

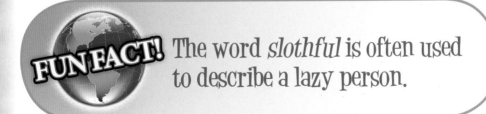

FUN FACT! The word *slothful* is often used to describe a lazy person.

It can be very difficult to spot a sloth if it does not want to be seen.

CHAPTER 3

Life in the Treetops

Sloths spend almost all their time in trees. There, they lead a mostly solitary lifestyle, rarely interacting with other sloths. Most of their time is spent sleeping. In fact, a sloth might sleep up to 20 hours per day. It is mainly active during the night, when it is less likely to be seen by predators.

The one thing a sloth does not do in the treetops is go to the bathroom. When a sloth needs to relieve itself, it waits for a safe opportunity and climbs down to the forest floor. There, it uses its claws to dig a hole in the ground, in which it buries its droppings. This process takes a long time and exposes the sloth to danger. As a result, sloths urinate and defecate only once about every one to two weeks. This is generally the only time a sloth is on the ground.

Sleeping is one of a sloth's main activities.

Time to Mate

Though adult sloths usually keep their distance from one another, they are not shy about getting together when it is time to mate. The mating habits of sloths vary from species to species. For example, brown-throated three-toed sloths mate with just one other sloth each season. Maned three-toed sloths, on the other hand, might mate with several partners during a season.

Generally, a female sloth makes noises to let nearby males know when she is ready to mate. The males might compete with one another for her attention. The female might make her choice based on the size or fur color of the rival males.

Like almost everything else they do, sloths mate and give birth while hanging from branches. Baby three-toed sloths are born around five to six months after their parents mate. Baby two-toed sloths take around twice as long to be born. In all sloth species, the mother gives birth to just a single baby at a time.

Baby sloths are fuzzy and helpless.

Growing and Changing

Male sloths do not help females raise their babies. However, mother sloths are able to provide plenty of care on their own. Newborn sloths look like smaller, fuzzier versions of adults. As soon as it is born, a baby sloth climbs onto its mother's belly. It stays there for several weeks or even months, depending on the species. As the mother travels through the forest, her baby rides along. Like other mammals, sloths feed their babies by providing milk from their bodies.

As a baby gets older and stronger, it learns to climb on its own. It also begins to eat leaves instead of milk. Once the young sloth is ready to fend for itself, its mother leaves it behind. For different species, this can take anywhere from two months to almost a year.

After about two to three years, a young sloth is ready to mate and have babies of its own. Depending on its species and its ability to stay away from harm, it will likely live for more than 20 years.

Mother sloths move carefully so their babies do not fall as they travel together.

CHAPTER 4

Ancient Animals

Sloths and their **ancestors** have been living on Earth for a very long time. Between 25 million and 4 million years ago, a wide range of sloth species lived throughout what are now North America, Central America, and South America. These ancient animals became **extinct** long ago. However, scientists have learned a lot about them by studying **fossils**.

Most ancient sloths lived much differently from the sloths we know today. Many of them lived on the ground instead of in the trees. Some ancient ground sloths lived as far north as Alaska and Canada. Other ancient sloths lived along the coasts of South America. These sloths spent almost all their time underwater. They dove down to the ocean floor to eat the sea plants growing there.

Some ancient ground sloths were very large.

Gigantic Ancestors

One of the most famous ancestors of today's sloths is *Megatherium*. Also known as the giant sloth, this humongous animal was roughly the size of a modern elephant. Its body was around 20 feet (6 meters) long, and it weighed 2 to 3 tons (1,814 to 2,722 kg). Its claws measured up to 20 inches (51 cm) long. This massive sloth lived between 2.6 million and 11,700 years ago. It became extinct around the time humans first started settling in the Americas.

Despite its enormous size, *Megatherium* had a lot in common with its modern relatives. For example, it lived in South America and ate mostly leaves and other plant parts. It also had long, powerful limbs with lengthy, curved claws at the ends. However, its lifestyle was very different from today's sloths. Instead of climbing trees, *Megatherium* spent all its time on the ground. Its powerful legs even allowed it to stand up tall and reach leaves on branches above.

Megatherium *may have looked something like this illustration.*

Today's Sloths

Scientists organize the sloth species still living today into two genera. One genus contains the two-toed sloth species. The other is made up of the three-toed sloths. There are only two species of two-toed sloths. They are the southern two-toed sloth and the Hoffmann's two-toed sloth. The species have slight physical differences. For example, the southern two-toed sloth has dark markings on the fur of its shoulders and arms, but the other species does not.

There are four species in the three-toed sloth genus. The pygmy three-toed sloth is a small species that lives on a single island near Panama. The maned sloth lives along the coast of Brazil. It is named for the long fur around its neck and shoulders. The pale-throated sloth and brown-throated sloth both live in rain forests throughout much of South America and Central America. They get their names from the color of fur along their throats and heads.

The three-toed pygmy sloth was first recognized as a separate species in 2001.

A Modern Relative

Sloths' closest living relatives are anteaters. Though these animals might not look much alike at first glance, they are actually both members of the **order** Pilosa. Like sloths, anteaters are found in parts of South America and Central America. They also range as far north as southern Mexico. These animals have a unique appearance that shares some features with their sloth cousins. For example, they have long, shaggy fur. Some anteaters even live in trees like sloths do. Others, such as the giant anteater, spend all their time on the ground.

An anteater's most distinctive features are its long, narrow face and lengthy tongue. These help it prey upon its favorite food: insects. Ants and termites make up the majority of an anteater's diet. Like sloths, anteaters have long claws on their feet. The anteater uses these claws to rip holes in insect mounds. It then sticks its face inside and uses its long, sticky tongue to scoop up mouthfuls of food.

Anteaters called tamanduas can climb trees much like sloths do.

CHAPTER 5

Sharing Space with Sloths

Like all living things, sloths play many important roles in their natural environments. For example, they are an important food source for some predators. Their fur is home to moths and other insects. Even their droppings are important, providing nutrients to plants, insects, and other life-forms.

Unfortunately, sloths are disappearing from many parts of the world. Several species are threatened or even endangered. If their situation does not improve, they could soon become extinct. This would in turn cause major problems for the countless other species that depend on sloths for survival.

Most of the dangers sloths face are a result of human activity. Even though there are laws in place to protect these animals, some people hunt them illegally for their meat. Other people capture sloths and try to keep them as pets. Such actions add to the big problems these animals are already facing.

A man helps a sloth return to its home after it fell to the ground.

Disappearing Homes

The biggest threat to sloths comes from habitat loss. In recent years, the rain forests that are homes to sloths have been rapidly disappearing. This is almost entirely because of human activity, such as logging. People are cutting down more and more trees to make wood and paper products. The growth of human settlements is another cause of habitat loss. Houses, businesses, and farmland are taking up space that was once home to sloths and other forest dwellers.

Roads are another problem for sloths. Because they are not good at traveling on the ground, it is very difficult for sloths to cross roads that run through their habitats. This can leave them boxed into much smaller areas than they need to survive. These animals might not have enough room to search for food. They might also be cut off from potential mates. This prevents them from reproducing and increasing their already shrinking population.

Logging activities in rain forests are a major problem for sloths and many other animals.

Looking Ahead

There is still a lot to learn about sloths and the way they live. Because they live deep inside dense forests and are hard to spot, it can be difficult to observe them in the wild. In addition, it is difficult to keep most types of sloths healthy in captivity. This means that it is just as hard to study them in zoos and other human-made environments as it is to see them up close in their natural habitats. It also makes it hard to help save sloths using captive breeding programs.

As scientists continue to study sloths and their rain forest homes, conservationists will work to protect these incredible animals from further harm. In the meantime, there are things that everyone can do to help prevent rain forests from continuing to shrink. For example, we can try to use fewer paper products. We can work to educate others about the importance of sloths and other rain forest species. With a little luck, these actions will help to ensure that sloths have a safe, healthy future.

A worker weighs a young sloth at a sanctuary in Costa Rica.

Words to Know

algae (AL-jee) — small plants without roots or stems that grow mainly in water

ancestors (AN-ses-turz) — ancient animal species that are related to modern species

breeding (BREED-ing) — mating and giving birth to young

camouflage (KAM-o-flaj) — coloring or body shape that allows an animal to blend in with its surroundings

captivity (kap-TIV-i-tee) — the condition of being held or trapped by people

conservationists (kon-sur-VAY-shun-ists) — people who work to protect an environment and the living things in it

defecate (DEF-uh-kate) — to pass solid waste from the body

digest (dye-JEST) — to break down food in the organs of digestion so that it can be absorbed into the blood and used by the body

endangered (en-DAYN-jurd) — at risk of becoming extinct, usually because of human activity

extinct (ik-STINGKT) — no longer found alive

fossils (FOSS-uhlz) — the hardened remains of prehistoric plants and animals

genera (JEN-ur-uh) — groups of related plants or animals that are larger than species but smaller than families

grooms (GROOMZ) — brushes and cleans

habitats (HAB-uh-tats) — places where an animal or a plant is usually found

mammals (MAM-uhlz) — warm-blooded animals that have hair or fur and usually give birth to live young

mate (MAYT) — to join together to produce babies

nutrients (NOO-tree-uhnts) — substances such as proteins, minerals, or vitamins that are needed by people, animals, and plants to stay strong and healthy

order (OR-duhr) — a category that groups different families of animals together according to similar traits that they share

predators (PREH-duh-turz) — animals that live by hunting other animals for food

prey (PRAY) — to hunt an animal for food

solitary (SOL-ih-tehr-ee) — preferring to live alone

species (SPEE-sheez) — one of the groups into which animals and plants of the same genus are divided

threatened (THRET-uhnd) — at risk of becoming endangered

urinate (YUR-uh-nate) — to pass liquid waste from the body

Habitat Map

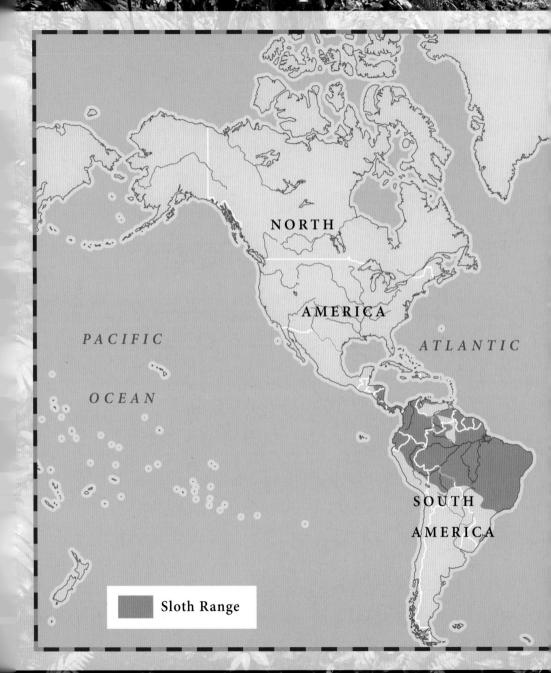

NORTH

AMERICA

PACIFIC

OCEAN

ATLANTIC

SOUTH

AMERICA

Sloth Range

ARCTIC OCEAN

EUROPE

ASIA

AFRICA

PACIFIC OCEAN

OCEAN

INDIAN OCEAN

AUSTRALIA

Find Out More

Books

Gray, Susan Heinrichs. *Megatherium*. Chanhassen, MN: Child's World, 2005.

Zabludoff, Marc. *Giant Ground Sloth*. New York: Marshall Cavendish Benchmark, 2010.

Visit this Scholastic Web site for more information on sloths:
www.factsfornow.scholastic.com
Enter the keyword **Sloths**

Index

Page numbers in *italics* indicate a photograph or map.

About the Author

Josh Gregory has written more than 80 books covering a wide range of subjects. He received a BA from the University of Missouri–Columbia. He works as a children's book editor and lives in Chicago, Illinois.